STUDENT
OF THE GAME

A STORYTELLER'S SOUL

Copyright: 1-14913934851

Spoken Word Memoir

EXCLUSIVE AUDIOBOOK EXPERIENCE

Opening Remarks:

BKS Publishing Presents:

Student of the Game

A Storyteller's SOUL

Spoken Word Memoir

Written by

Brandon 'SOUL COLE' Coleman

I welcome you as the reader to this safe space intentionally curated to reflect the Love & Light from within my vessel to speak to your heart & soul.

I invite you to consider embarkin' on this journey releasin' any expectations that you may have, & come w/ an open mind & heart to receive all that is for you from the divine.

W/ your consent, may the vibration of these words resonate deeply as it penetrates the surface level to reach the spirit of oneness that rests within, now let the story begin.

CHAPTER 1
Intro: Created Player

Video games, ice in your veins

popular names, Lebron James!

Physically gifted, God assisted.

All attributes lifted 99 scripted,

across the board

& countless awards, built tough like Ford's.

Reapin' the rewards of the sacrifice,

practice late @ nights.

Constantly measurin' your weight & height,

to see if you measure up to standards that exceed

expectations, to handle in game situations,

by focusin' your concentration

through practicin' meditation.

Superstar activation,

MyPlayer has been created

by the Creator of all creation.

Formed from the dust of the ground,

breathin' life into my crown,

through my nose as the inhale flows &

circulates the exhale out through my toes.

Standin' on business, you are here to witness

the truth bein' told as this story unfolds.

Aséo

CHAPTER 2
Student of The Game

They say life is a game, so focus your aim

as you build your frame, workin' through any shame

attached to your name.

Don't play for the fame, just learn from your pain & smile

through the rain,

remember you are a student of the game.

They say when the student is ready

the teacher will appear,

so be prepared for a dynamic shift in your atmosphere.

For your guide is here, near & dear to your heart,

that's where the first lesson starts.

Remindin' you that Love is the key

to unlock trú divinity within thee to infinity & beyond.

Your next lesson is to respond w/ poise in the noise.

As distractions come & go,

just as your thoughts continue to flow

in & out of your mind.

The game is played one breath @ a time.

So here is your invitation

to arrive in the present moment.

Another reason for you to own it,

so submit your application for your early enrollment.

As a student of the game of life,

here's a word of advice - you are both

the mentee & the mentor,

the player & the coach,

the rookie & the vet

- all one in the same.

Just as you & I are connected beyond space & time.

The last lesson is to have a beginner's state of mind.

So everytime you hear this line, you feel this rhyme.

You are a lifelong learner,

so continue to allow your mind to grow & expand knowin'

things won't always go accordin' to your plans & that's okay.

Over time you will evolve & adapt as a

Student of the Game

I end this poem w/ a (snap).

No Thanos, but that's a wrap.

Asè

CHAPTER 3
SOUL Tapped In

What if I told you my journey of tappin' in

started way back when,

before then I knew what was even happenin'?

A seed was planted but the route was slanted

& I took it for granted, droppin' the shuffle ball change.

Although tap dancin' felt strange,

Happy Feet expanded my range.

Then Savion became an artistic name

for me to study his game.

I appreciate Ms. King for lettin' me do my thang.

Gave me permission to let my feet sang, out loud.

I know that she is proud.

Even though I stumble you won't hear me Mumble,

I get tired of bein' humble.

As I channel this straight from the heart of the jungle,

all I can hear is rumble young man rumble!

Listenin' to the bee's as they bumble,

I'm tappin' in w/ the birds & the trees,

the God within.

If you want to win put Cole in

& watch him spin.

That fancy footworkin'.

He tip toein' w/ two feet down,

playin' in the pros now.

Came along ways from dem highschool grounds.

Steppin' on stage, now you've done turned the page

in this book, made them take a second look

@ how far you've come.

Feels like the story has just begun.

Connected to the One has been

ear-openin', oops I meant eye-openin'

matter of fact I meant boffum dem.

It's all a part of the growth in him.

Practicin' mindfulness got him so tapped in,

look @ him toe-tappin' up the sideline

in the white shoes w/ an electric cruise

just popped a fuse.

Activatin' Christ views

this is breakin' news, of a hidden talent

of a fine-art,

God bless his heart, from start to finish.

His souls replenished, its a photo finish.

It goes under review& the call stands

as the umpire raises both his hands

to confirm to the fans,

so do your touchdown dance.

It is not by chance that you are SOUL tapped in.

Don't put my feet to the test.

I know I'm the best, I said it w/ my chest,

I'm up there w/ the rest ...

Mr. Bill Bojangles, Sir Charles Coles, The Great Gregory Hines

& between these lines

embedded spiritual signs.

Time to close these blinds,

Somebody (ring my chimes)

Asé

CHAPTER 4
Eye in The Sky

They say the eye in the sky don't lie, I wonder why?

I've always been a curious kinda guy,

that knows he can fly w/ a birds eye view.

So let me help you see this 3rd eye through.

As we breakdown the tape,

let's get your mind in shape.

It's nowhere to escape, it's no time to waste.

If you wanna be great it's not up for debate.

So eliminate the illusion & cut out the confusion

this is how to be a pro, I'm here to let you know

from experience, I've seen it all before.

Don't take it personal, you gotta be coachable

to train your eyes to know what you're lookin' for.

There is an art to takin' notes, some may do the most

but find what works for you,

payin' attention to the details is a clue.

This will help you improve your performance, this is trú.

I appreciate the different perspectives

& multiple points of view. Just like the refs do,

when a play is under review, frame by frame

watchin' the film of the game of life.

Sometimes you roll the dice thinkin' you are nice,

are you willin' to pay the price

bein' exposed in the light... or in a dark room,

you think it's night, w/ a laser pen that can write

& points out or highlights, askin' can you

identify the Mike? Like check 1, 2.

What do you do when nobody is watchin' you,

testin' your character trú? Knowin' Jah sees you

in all that you do.

See, the I in I is the eye in the sky,

The same one that's on the sparrow

The focus is sharp & narrow.

Flexible - flex the bow w/ an arrow

To guide you in the direction

to enhance your connection,

it's not about perfection.

More about progression

keep learnin' your lessons

from these film study sessions.

This is a teach tape profession,

your blindspot I'm addressin'.

No Usher but I'm confessin',

the sun, stars & the moon are expressin',

divinity that is refreshin'.

Send you in motion, that's window dressin',

If you know, you know or you guessin'?

(Hahaaa)

The eye in the sky is a blessin'.

(Mhmmm)

Asé

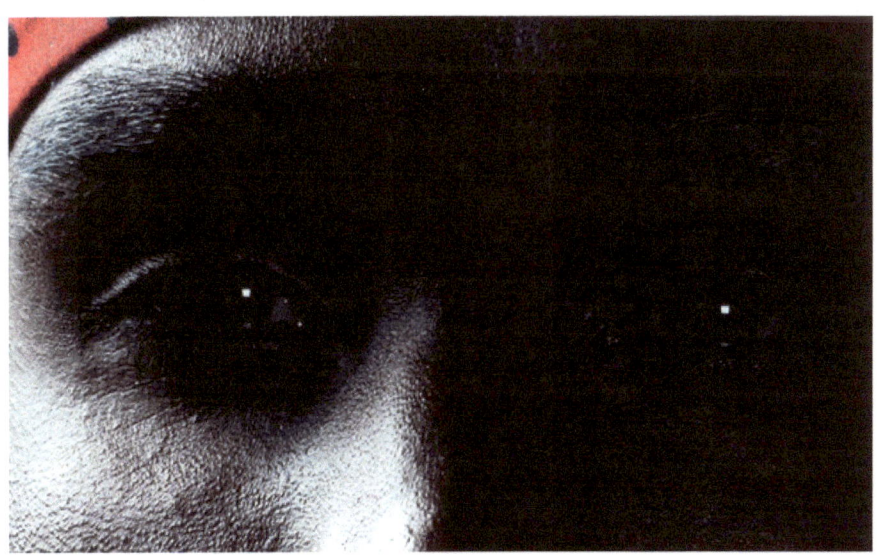

CHAPTER 5
Last of the Mohicans

A classic storyline from the past,

a movie that shed light through a glass.

A father & son bond over this movie early on.

I won't go to deep into the plot, I know it can be a lot.

So I open my book & I jot

this connection down to the spot,

of a full circle moment.

I gotta share how I became aware

stories like this are rare,

so listen up as I prepare

to take you on this journey.

Paintin' a motion picture w/ my words

citin' sacred scriptures w/ this verse

"all things work together for good

to them that love God

to them who are called accordin' to his purpose"

even when I was called, I didn't answer

because I was nervous.

I left school early on purpose, to enter the draft

chasin' the surface level respect

so goin' undrafted I didn't expect.

Can you imagine the emotional wreck?

I didn't even have time to reflect.

Just had time to accept, it is what it is.

Time to go handle my biz like show

even doe the odds were against me, you know.

To be the last man standin' from my class

God was w/ me, never left me nor forsake me.

The script was already written,

the characters Great like Britain.

Fightin' alongside the Native American tribe

w/ honor & pride, til the French came to divide

w/ deceit & lies.

In this film, I'm givin' main character vibes

& besides the NFL stands for — Not For Long.

So to my surprise I looked up & everybody

was gone. Some on different teams,

some went north of the border & the rest I

shrug my shoulders, now I'm 4 years older

a veteran, No Limit Soldier.

A classic, what I told ya.

Standin' tall like magnolia.

Chingachgook,

Last of the Mohicans.

My Light is bright as a beacon.

This is the truth that I'm speakin',

my red-tail feather I'm keepin'.

Can you grasp what I'm preachin'?

I'm the Last of the Mohicans!

Asé

CHAPTER 6
The Evolution

A story I desire to tell,

channelin' deep from within my well,

vibratin' through every cell w/ innocence.

In a sense, I can smell, taste, touch, hear & see,

the imminent evolution of me, of we, of all of thee above as so

below, allow this story to flow

as I continue to grow & adapt, avoidin' the trap of

remainin' the same.

Learnin' how to respond to change,

expandin' my range

as I reach for the stars, to pull up these bars.

Workin' out the fears & tears

choked up over all these years.

Time to shift the gears, to a new dimension

a spiritual ascension, manifestin' intentions.

Now that I have your undivided attention,

don't let me forget to mention, to release all the tension

& let go of the conditionin' in your spirit, body, & mind,

knowin' that they are all intertwined w/ the divine.

Your human design is beyond space & time.

It cannot be confined, in fact scriptures says that,

"be not conformed to this world but be ye transformed by the

renewin' of your mind".

If ye seek, ye shall find all that is aligned

for the advancement of your bein', the enhancement of your

seein' is essentially freein' you to become who've you

been called to be & honestly it is a necessity for your

longevity to increase

your vitality as you progress through this reality,

upgradin' your mentality,

as you remember the journey has no end.

Only the beginnin' so keep those wheels spinnin'.

As you move through each phase,

navigatin' this maze, the evolution will amaze

the man from the cave

he will say that you are brave,

as you pass by & (wave)

as the sound of the ocean plays

to the beat of my drum.

The evolution is a return to the One.

This poem is done!

Asé

CHAPTER 7
Gentle Giants

(Fee - Fi - Fo - Fum) known as a gentle giant to some,

but for most who see a melanated man you see,

who stands as tall as a tree

w/ a divine God body physique

find it hard to believe the fruits of the spirit are

grounded in thee,

beneath the soil rooted up to align his Crown Royal.

Society will judge his book by his cover &

overlook the compassionate lover,

the empathy he discovers & kindness that hovers his

energetic aura,

an Avatar from planet Pandora.

Walkin' smooth w/ a feather in his fedora.

A trú classic gentleman who keeps it simple man

don't forget his toothpick man.

A physical specimen who is non-aggressive man

please don't test this man

& take his kindness for weakness,

respect his uniqueness & honor

the practice of meekness.

In the presence of a gentle giant,

a big baby if you will whose mood is tranquil.

A man's best friend is a dog they say,

so I got a cane corso & I named him Ace.

A pure breed indeed, he stuck to his creed,

his brindle coat even matched me.

We both shared complimentary energy,

A gentle giant you see.

Intimidated by his size & his bark,

our bond was sealed from the start,

almost made the three year mark

before we had to sadly depart,

it crushed my Tony Stark heart.

The hardest thang I ever had to do

was to surrender my rights to you.

See the pandemic had came & that changed the game

& I could no longer provide the same.

So I did what was best for you @ that moment in time.

That's how I eventually came to find this peace of mind.

My emotions were far to real & I needed to feel

In order for me to heal.

I know we always connected but still,

See Imma gentle giant for real,

not ashamed to verbally express my pain

as tears fell from my face like rain.

May you be loved.

May you be happy.

May you be well.

May you be @ peace.

May you be safe.

Know that you will always be my Ace

& that will always bring a smile to my face.

Asé

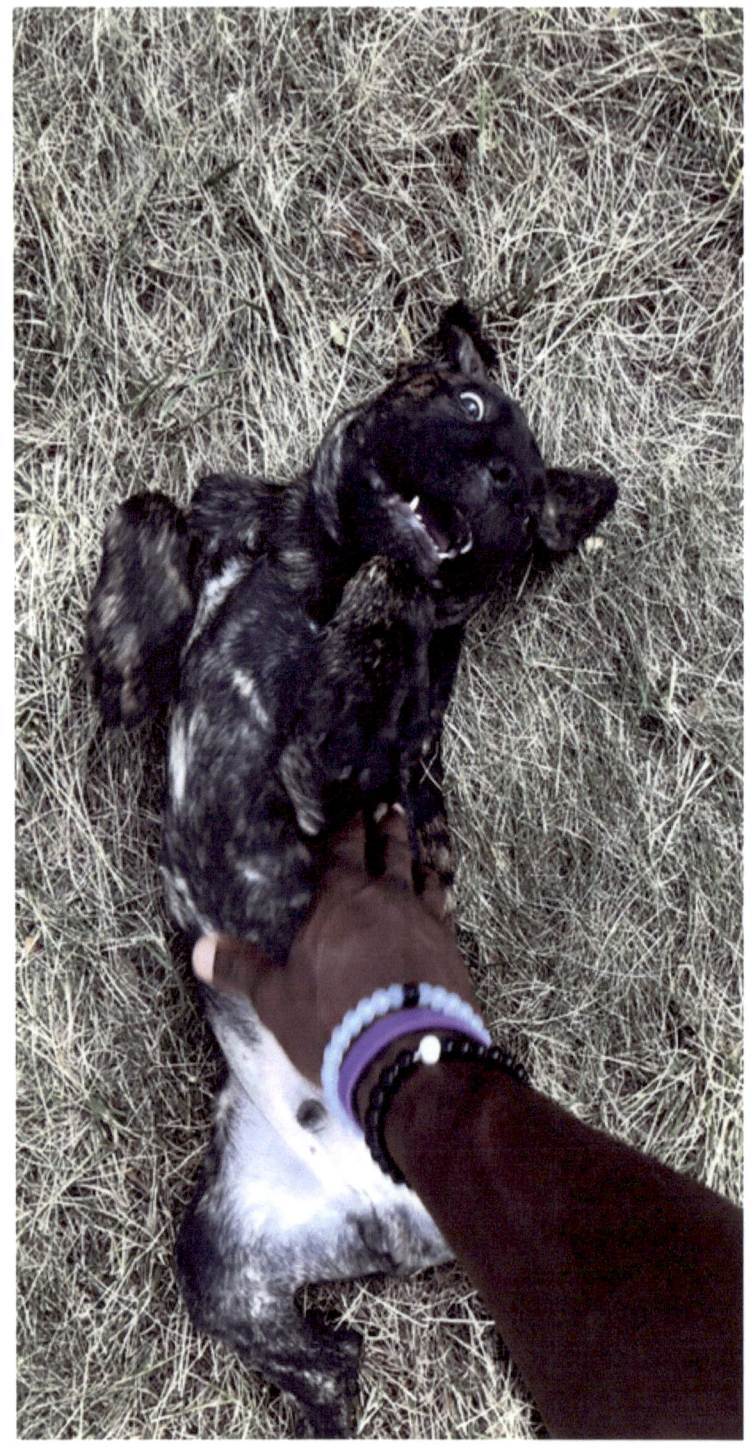

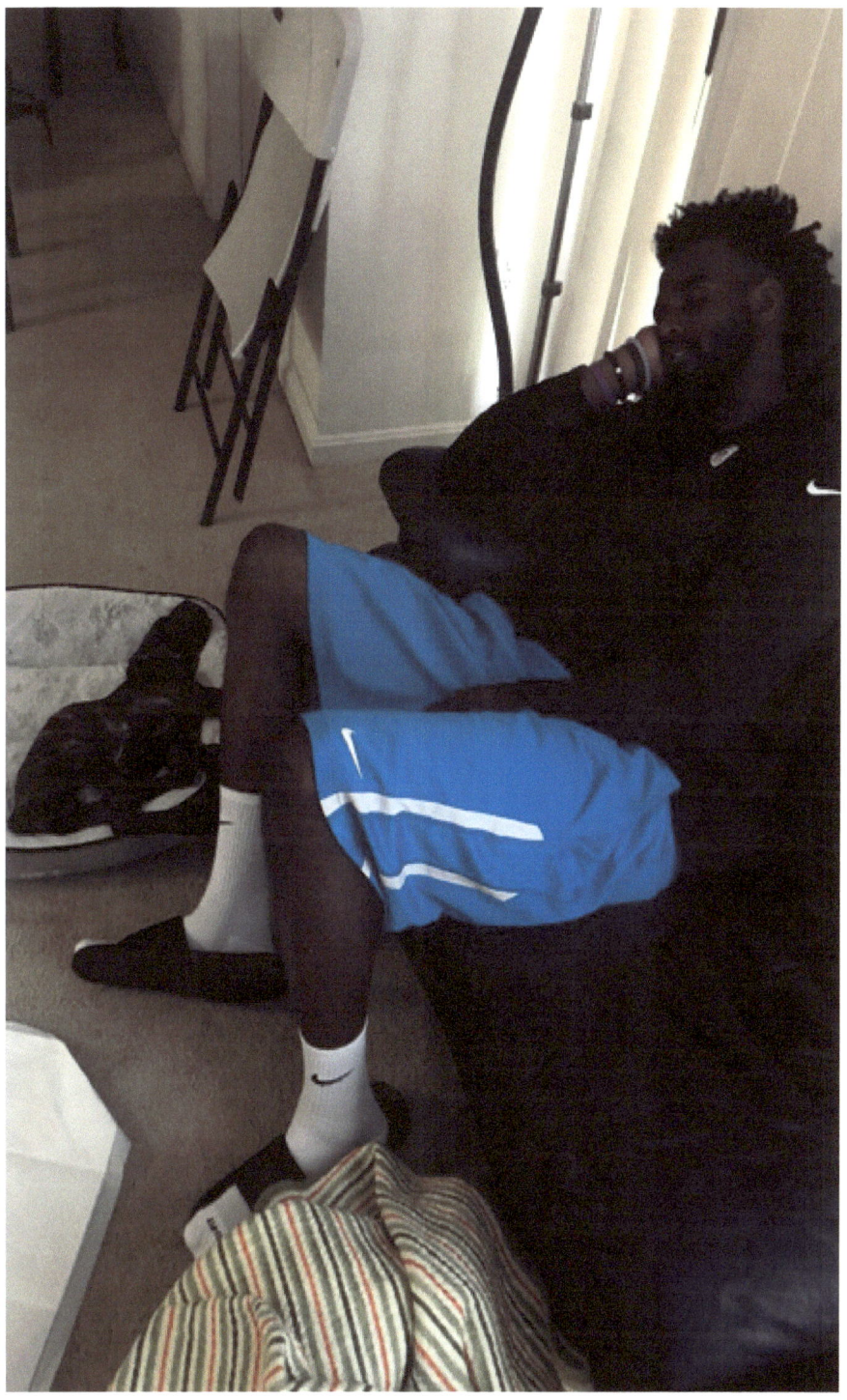

CHAPTER 8
JUNGLE KING

I call in my spirit animals to sound thee alarm throughout

nature's permaculture farm.

I come in peace, so do me no harm.

I'm talkin' to you Sheer-Khan.

As I channel this charm, no lucky leprechaun.

I'm up @ the break of dawn, runnin' this marathon called

life. In the heart of the jungle,

I take a page out of your book.

A man cub standin' down by the brook,

or a young Simba as he takes a second look,

down into the water, he was shook.

To see Mufasa in thee, to remind you of who you are!

You are the King of the Jungle, so even if you stumble,

don't let a Scar lessen your confidence.

Simply learn the lesson, it's common sense.

The bare necessities I recommence.

In other words, a minimalist as you journey

through these sacred lands

some hot like dessert sands,

feel the energy charge through your hands.

The circle of life all came trú when you stayed

@ Hotel Balu.

That's when you knew you felt right @ home

w/ Rafiki's tree surrounded by howler monkeys,

I'm talkin' to you Mowgli.

Can't you see, your inner child @ play

intertwinin' movies along the way.

Papa Bear & his prickly pear

or Timon & Pumba, such a compellin' pair.

I dare you to stare into the Jungle King's glare.

SOUL enemies beware, the wolfpack got my back.

I'm returnin' home to Pride Rock & that's a fact.

To make a SOUL Impact to be exact. To be the

Light I was called to be.

It's a privilege for me to see spiritually how Jah

chooses to speak to me & through me,

as I surrender to thee & let thy will be done

& thy Kingdom come,

my buffalo drum circle calls the ancestors in

as the ceremony (begins).

We ask forgiveness for our sins,

then celebrate our wins.

Honorin' the God within,

who knows beginnin' from the end.

This story was already locked in,

I just had to call it in.

Asé

CHAPTER 9
"Divine Time"
Break The Stigma

May these words offer healin' vibrations,

servin' refreshin' inspiration,

w/ ab-*soul*-ute motivation.

As I channel this co-creation,

to impact generations amongst many nations ... It's okay

not to be okay! I know it sounds cliché,

we gon break the stigma anyway.

By normalizin' the conversation, I'll lead the way

w/ the art of storytellin', I say, my mental health journey

started back in the day.

A freshman in Piscataway, New Jersey.

Big man on campus, the gridiron was my canvas.

Redshirt came & I didn't have the answers.

Depression started to sink in, self doubt is all I'm thinkin',

before I knew it the next year came from blinkin'.

I'm finally playin' but I'm stinkin'.

I'm heated, I can't even catch a cold.

A sports psychiatrist was recommended but he was old

& white, not an ounce of athleticism in sight.

I knew that wasn't right, I left & didn't think twice.

@ the time I thought it was a sign of weakness,

now I'm back in the lab workin' on my craft

suppressin' the feelings that I had.

I ain't got time to feel sad.

Strap on the shoulder pads

keep it movin' now I'm groovin'

my game steady improvin'

but wait... there's more,

a torn meniscus was (knocking) at my door,

brought me down to the floor, didn't have

the same confidence as before.

Adversity in life you can't ignore.

My senior year I played it sore.

I still battled & went to war.

Nobody can question my toughness, that's for sure.

Fast forward to the draft, I aint eem get picked last!

All I felt was shame had to charge it to the game,

it is what it is, what you gon do cry about it?

Cuz that's what I did. It's okay to cry,

it's a natural release of energy off the line
of scrimmage.

I'm not concerned about my image,

I'm more anxious about bein' released,

if I can keep it a beast, if I can keep it a bean,

you know what I mean, my job security ain't clean.

I'm gettin' it out the mud, sweat, tears & blood.

This practice period is thud!

That means keep em' up,

stay off the ground, this is my profession now.

I'm breakin' this stigma all the way down.

Pound for pound.

Round for round.

Even sound for sound.

Advocatin' all around.

See 2018 it all came crashin' down on me.

Off season surgeries on my neck & on my hip,

I'm questionin' — who wrote this script?

On who depression don't exist,

I don't want to hear that shit!

How I'm gon bounce back from this?

Thinkin' I can't go out like this.

What made it even worse I had to keep it all on the low.

The public ain't eem know,

this was a private show.

I ain't have the tools in place to help me navigate it doe.

Sufferin' in silence is a heavy burden to carry that weight alone

I promise you, you are not alone.

I struggled to receive the love & support from my own home.

This level of vulnerability I never known,

all this trauma trapped inside my bones

my pride won't let me pick up the phone

& ask for help... Why?

Because I'm conditioned to sayin' — I'll get it myself.

I rehabbed as hard as the little engine that could

hopeful that I would, get another chance

to have this last dance, to display my romance

for this game I gave my heart,

@ the start I was 6, just a kid in the mix

now retired @ 26.

Check the score on the board game

I'm onto the next play mentality.

Later that year my tippin' point crushed my reality,

when my grandfather transitioned to immortality.

I finally buckle down & agree to go to therapy

but it wasn't that easy to find someone to relate to me.

It was a trial & error you see.

I needed a safe space to be free unapologetically

to express my full range of emotions w/ transparency.

See, that doesn't make me less of a man,

don't you inner-stand you can't duck from doin' that

real work forever.

Some shit you gon uncover you may not be ready for,

however you can storm any weather & weather every

storm that will form.

This is a new norm,

I'm usin' my platform

to transform w/ a Shockwave,

I'm Bumble Bee brave,

Myself, I forgave.

My mental health I had to save,

from goin' off the deep end.

yeah, suicide ideation was creepin'.

Checked into a rehab facility for 30 days

& all I'm thinkin' is what others are goin' to say if they find out
I went to a shrink man.

If suicide is somethin' you thinkin',
dial 9-8-8

to get you LinkedIn.

Know that help is on the way.

Live to Love another day,

your life is worth livin' I say.

We set free generational curses through these verses

overcomin' the pain bein' a Student of the Game,

breakin' these chains & the stigma.

So misunderstood but what's a world without enigma?

Weezy F. Baby

& the F is for your feelings that are validated

my superpowers - animated,

emotional intelligence - activated,

the taboo - eliminated, evaporated,

w/ all the love I generated,

intentionally illustrated

through representation & relatability,

R&R

to shine a light on the darkness.

As we journey through the highs & the lows,

the ebbs & the flows.

Let's take a moment to follow the breath

in through the nose... (inhale)

& observe it as it goes

out through the mouth ... (exhale)

That's a lot to digest & process

w/ the hopes to reduce stress.

Sending Peace & Love,

always

Jah Bless.

Asé-Buttah-Bae-namasté

have a blessed day & night,

everythin' is gonna be alright.

Poem.

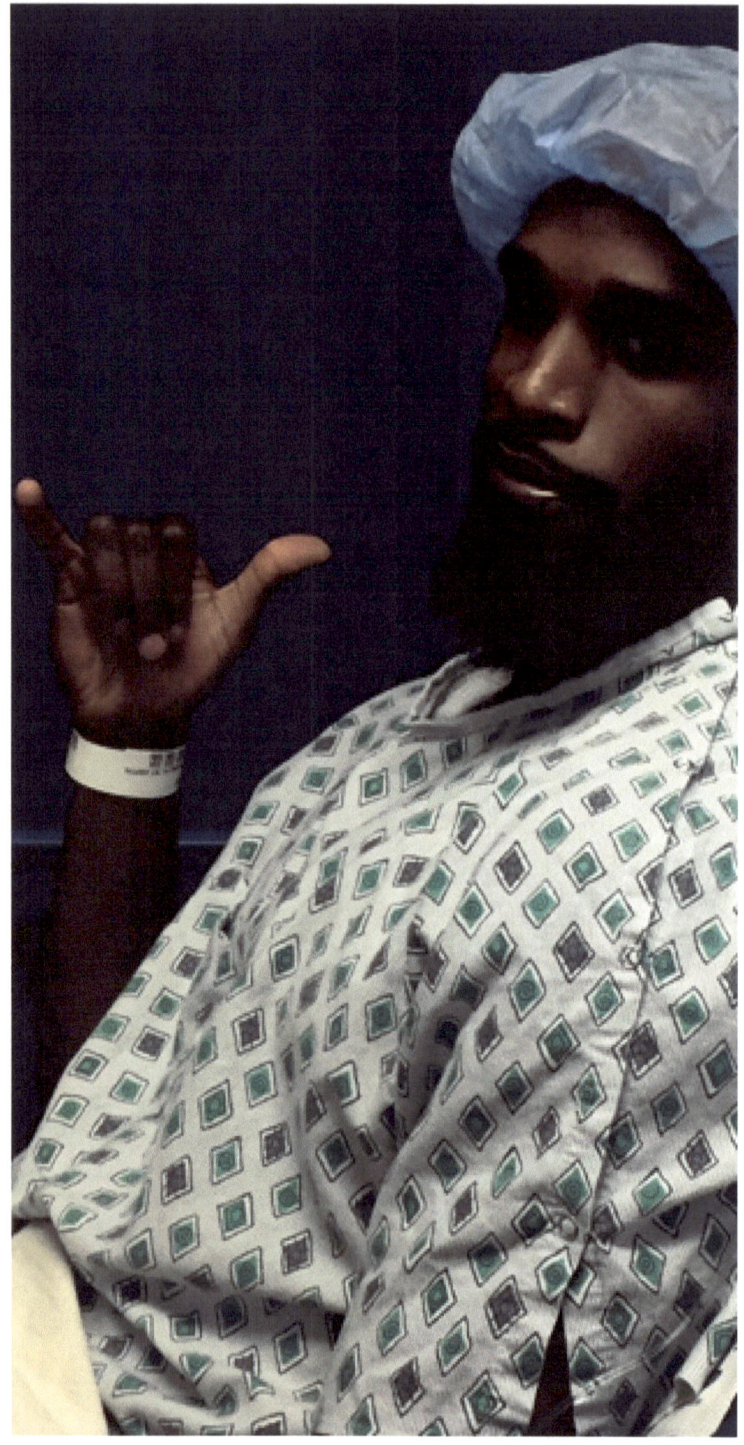

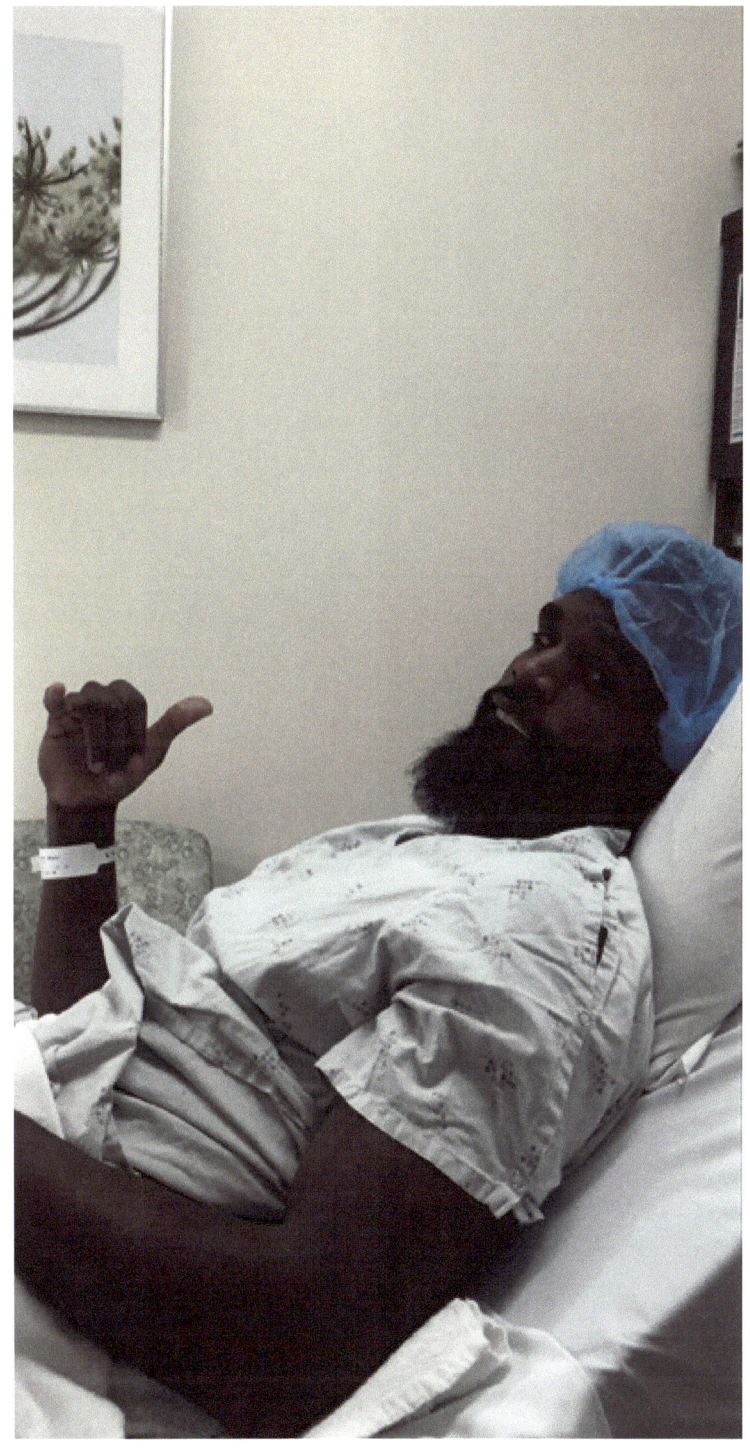

Acknowledgements
& Reflections:

This project is a dedication to my future self-I am profoundly proud of you & deeply in love w/ every version of you that has been & will be as you continue to evolve.

First & foremost, all praises to the Most High, Yahweh, my Lord & Savior, Yeshua, who has gifted me the ability to share these downloads from my spirit, in my most authentic & divine expression. This story book is more than a collection of words that rhyme; it is a testament to my spiritual journey that is far from linear which I am honored to share.

I extend my heartfelt gratitude to my family, my core foundation, & of course the Fantastic Four formulation, who has remained steadfast by my side through every chapter of my life. your support has been my anchor & my guidin' light.

To my late grandparents & great-grandmother, whose spirits continue to guide & protect me every day, may you continue to shine your love over me from the heavens above.
You are missed beyond words, just know your influence remains an undeniable part of who I am & aspire to be.

The essence of this book speaks to resilience-the message is clear: when life breaks you down, it is not to defeat you, but to prepare you for your breakthrough. The cracks in your armor that form from our imperfections are a safe space for the Light to shine through offerin' hope & peace that surpasses all understandin'.

By focusin' on self-awareness & recognizin' the profound power w/ our own voices, it is about findin' victory in a voice that is uniquely yours-a sound that resonates truth & authenticity. Throughout my journey, w/ its peaks & valleys,

I have tapped into my own vibration, one that I've always known, which I regard as one of my superpowers.

As a trú storyteller it is my intention that these pages fulfill my divine assignment to inspire ONE, empower ONE, equip just ONE soul as a servant leader for the Kingdom of God's glory as I share these sacred stories w/ anointed authority. I give thanks to everyone who has walked this path w/ me. your presence in my life has enriched my journey, & for that, I am eternally grateful.

Thank you for tappin' in. May you always **remember** to harness the power of your voice w/ each breath & know that every challenge is a steppin' stone to greater heights.

Until we practice again,

I impart to you Peace & Love from my highest self above,

Aséo

Hasta Luego

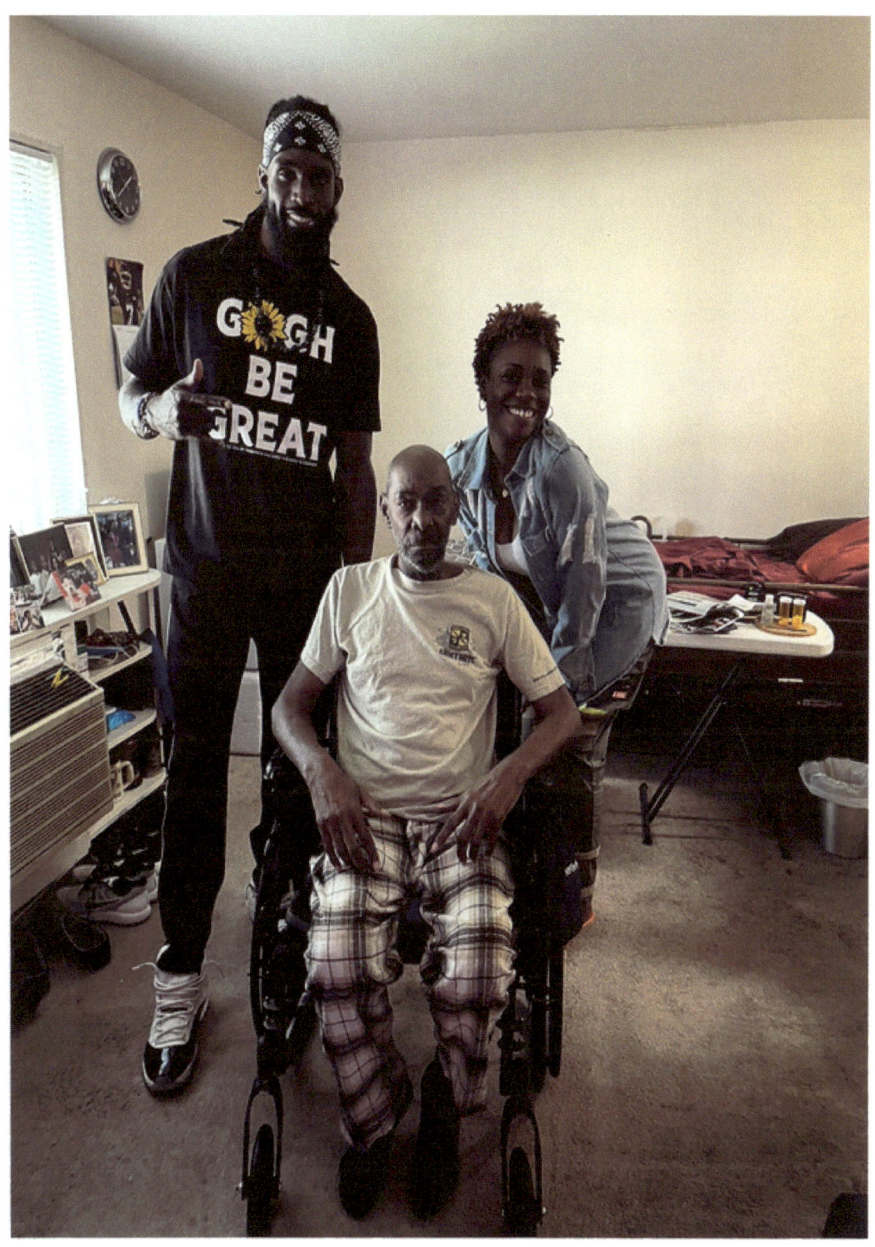

www.ingramcontent.com/pod-product-compliance
Lightning Source LLC
Chambersburg PA
CBHW040855120626
46551CB00001B/29